Day & Night

A 30 Day
Praise & Worship Journey

Justin McGowan

Justin McGowan
2556 Moore's Road
Seaman, OH 45679
www.church180.org

This book is dedicated to all those who are hungry for more of Him; to those who are thirsty for the Presence of The Lord. May we enter into His glorious throne room and bask in His Glory. To those who long to declare His holiness, I dedicate this book to you.

DAY ONE

*"But the time is coming—indeed it's here now—when true
worshipers will worship the Father in spirit and in truth. The
Father is looking for those who will worship him that way. For
God is Spirit, so those who worship him must worship in spirit
and in truth."*
John 4:24 NLT

Jesus laid it all out for the Samaritan woman. She had
questions and He had answers. What is the correct way to
worship?

Should we use video screens with the lyrics displayed or go
back to the traditional hymnal? Should we sing praise in a loud
voice lifted to Heaven or bow in quiet submission? Should we
utilize the talents of our congregation and have a full band or
only have a piano or organ? Yes, just like the Samaritan
woman, there are many of us who have questions as well.

What is worship that the Father finds acceptable? What are
His thoughts on this subject? As we embark on this 30-day

journey together we will discover what is pleasing to the Lord when it pertains to worshiping Him. We will dig into the Word and discover the Heart of our Precious Lord.

Interestingly, Jesus never answers those questions that we so eagerly ask. Is it okay to play drums in church? Is it okay to play electric guitar? Is it still acceptable to have only the organ? Maybe the problem is that we have been asking the wrong questions all along.

When the Samaritan woman asked about worship, Jesus never mentioned music at all! He never once spoke about the importance of starting a worship set out with an upbeat praise song to wake the crowd. He never once spoke on the idea that you must end the set with a slow worship song. Not once!

No, Jesus went straight to the heart of the matter. Those who worship the Father must worship in SPIRIT and in TRUTH. He even goes so far as to say that the Father is *looking* for those kinds of people!

You may be saying, *that's all good and well but how do I go about doing that?* I am glad you asked!

God is looking for those who will worship Him in spirit. To understand this, we must first understand what the spirit is.

Our spirit is not our soul. In our American culture we often interchange these two terms. They are not the same. Our soul is our mind, will, and emotions. These can be manipulated. They can be changed and often do many times daily. They can evolve over time.

Our spirit can only be changed by God. Our spirit is the essence of who we are. We cannot change it except by the wonder-working power of the Holy Spirit. It is us at our core. It is the part of ourselves that communes with God. The Holy Spirit of God speaks to this part of us. His Spirit bears witness with our spirit. This is where our worship should come from and our soul should follow suit. Our spirit should always be the leader when it comes to our soul. Not only that, but God has given us His Spirit which enables our spirit to respond to His Majesty.

Next, we have the matter of truth. How might we worship the Father in truth? Again, we must first lay some groundwork on for what truth is.

In John 14:6, Jesus said, "I am the way, the truth, and the life. No one can come to the Father except through me." In order to get to the Father, we must enter in through Jesus. Jesus is truth. If we have not become a follower of Christ, then we have no way of worshiping in the way that the Father desires.

Today, as you go throughout your day, remember that the Father is *looking* for those who will worship Him in *spirit* and in *truth*. His eye is going throughout the earth searching for these kinds of people. Are you one of them?

We have made things much more complicated than they really are. God's idea of true worship doesn't have anything to do with musical style or vocal ability. It has everything to do with our heart toward Him, His Word, and His Spirit.

Father, help us today to become one of those You are searching for. May we come before You and worship You in spirit and truth. Thank you for the opportunity to do this. Thank You, Jesus, for making the way. Holy Spirit, help us to commune with You and be led by You into the Throne Room of Heaven!
In Jesus' Name!

DAY TWO

*"And David was greatly distressed; for the people spake of
stoning him, because of the soul of all the people was grieved,
every man for his sons and daughters: but David encouraged
himself in the LORD his God."*
1 Samuel 30:6 KJV

Have you ever had one of those days where it seems that the
world is against you? You know the scenario; you sleep
through your alarm and are running 30 minutes behind. You're
finally ready to leave but cannot seem to find your left shoe.
You finally find your shoe but now you have a bigger issue—
where are the car keys? You're now 45 minutes behind
schedule only to discover that you are stuck behind a school
bus. By the time you arrive at the office, you wish you had just
taken a personal day. The only problem is that the boss is
expecting that report which was due an hour ago.

By now your emotions are running wild. You stop to get a
drink at the water cooler and bump into the talkative co-
worker. Your thoughts are racing. "Do they not know that I

have work to do? I am already behind and don't have time to be stopping to talk to you!"

You finally get through the day and arrive home. You crash onto the couch in hopes that you can just forget this day altogether. Just then your heart skips a beat. You forgot to pick the kids up from practice. You leap to your feet and wonder what you did to deserve this. By the time you return home you realize that you have spent the entire car ride yelling at the kids to be quiet, settle down, etc. You snap at your wife as you walk through the door. You have had a bad day and you're not in the mood for small talk.

You rush off to bed and get ready to do it all again tomorrow. You ask yourself a question. *Isn't life supposed to be so much more joyful than this?* Your guilty mind wallows away in the day's events as you slowly drift off to sleep.

We are all prone to having a bad day now and then. We have all been guilty of allowing our outward experience to influence our inward response. I have done this for sure. But is this the right response to have?

King David was in quite the predicament. When he arrived in Ziklag he was perplexed to learn that all the women and children had been captured and forced into slavery. His remaining men were angry towards him and sought to stone him. Talk about a bad day!

It would have been easy for David to fall into depression. It would have been easy for David to give in to anger and blame God for the events that had taken place. No one would have blamed him if he would have just given up hope and accepted this terrible fate. But what did he do?

The man who is responsible for writing many psalms of praise to God had a response that I am sure many in the world would find quite peculiar. *He encouraged himself in the Lord his God.* Even though it looked as though all was lost, he refused to allow this to define his response.

Yes, unlike the person who became frustrated, angry, and unkind when the day did not go as planned, David's inward response influenced his outward experience.

On those days when it feels that the whole world is against us, we can come to know that really the world is against us. But that shouldn't discourage us. Even though the world is against us, God is for us! Instead of turning to the world on "those" days, we should immediately turn to God! There was a time in my life when I would allow one tiny, little thing ruin my day. After several years of this I came across this story and realized that I didn't have to live this way. There is a better way!

When we have difficult days, our immediate response should always be to turn to God. When we begin to lift Him up He begins to lift us up. When we take our eyes off the temporary and begin to behold the glory of the One who is eternal our troubles begin to shrink.

David recovered all that he had lost and recovered the plunder left behind from the enemy. When we encourage ourselves in the Lord, we get back all the enemy tries to steal from us and more! We will always walk in victory when we always honor God!

Father, thank you for giving us the opportunity to be encouraged in You! I declare now that I will always look to You for my strength. My desire is to bring honor to You in my life. Let my eyes always look unto You. I praise You for what You've done! I worship You for Who You Are! All glory to You.
In Jesus' Name!

DAY THREE

"And they sang in a mighty chorus: 'Worthy is the Lamb who was slaughtered—to receive power and riches and wisdom and strength and honor and glory and blessing.'"
Revelation 5:12 NLT

John's Book of Revelation is probably the book of the Bible which incites more fear than any other. The imagery is astounding. It describes scenes that our physical minds can barely imagine. Great beasts covered with eyes, front and back, which have six wings also covered with eyes, front and back. John speaks of plagues being released onto the earth. He tells us of a large red dragon with seven heads, ten horns, and seven crowns on his heads. He paints us a picture of a beast rising out of the sea which looked like a leopard, but with feet like a bear and a mouth like a lion!

It is easy to see why so many fear this book! We often read about the great beasts and then lay the Bible down, refusing to read any further.

Many people like to pick a part this book and try to figure out when the end-times will take place exactly. I, on the other hand, have discovered that although these scenes are amazing to read about, the scenes of worship are much more stirring.

You see, to me, the book of Revelation is a big book of worship. It allows us a peek into the window of Heaven. It gives us a glimpse of the activities that will take place in the future and what is occurring right now—even as I write this; even as you read these words.

Revelation tells us that Heaven never ceases worshiping the One Who sits on the Throne. *And they rest not day and night, saying, Holy, holy, holy, Lord God Almighty, which was, and is, and is to come.* How incredible is that?

We read about the One seated upon the Throne. He is *as brilliant as gemstones—like jasper and carnelian. And the glow of an emerald encircles His Throne like a rainbow.* Can you imagine? How incredible is our God! Our Eternal King!

Chapter 5 tells us of a choir made up of saints and angels singing *Worthy is the Lamb who was slaughtered!* What an astounding song that is! I personally think that the scariest part of the entire book is the idea of missing out on the marvelous worship taking place!

Doesn't that make you long for the day when you are able to go before the Throne of God and worship Him? Well I have good news for you! You don't have to wait!

We can join in with Heaven's song now! We don't have to wait until we leave this world! We have been given the opportunity to lift our voice to the One Who saved us and do it today!

And then I heard every creature in heaven and on earth and under the earth and in the sea. They sang: "Blessing and honor and glory and power belong to one sitting on the throne and to the Lamb forever and ever."

While leading worship at my church there have been many occasions when I have felt prompted to sing out lyrics that weren't planned out by me; to sing lyrics different than those pre-planned and pre-written. Many times, I have found the Holy Spirit leading me to sing things like: *You Are worthy, our Lord and God. You created all things and they exist because You created them!* Sometimes I just feel the leading to sing *Holy, Holy, Holy!* When this occurs, I can sense in my spirit that the words aren't just bouncing from the four walls of our church and going no further than the ceiling. No, I can tangibly *feel* the song rising-up before the Throne in harmony with the song of heaven.

As I said before, we do not have to wait to join in with Heaven's Song. Why would we want to wait?

Today I encourage you to read the lyrics of the Song of Heaven given in Revelation and join in with your whole heart. Sing it out unto the One Who is worthy to receive all wealth and wisdom. Know that when you do this your song will rise-up and intermingle with the song being sung in Heaven!

Holy, holy, holy is the Lord God, Almighty—Who was, and is, and is to come! Worthy is the Lamb Who was slain to receive power, and riches, and wisdom! With Your Blood You purchased us for God!

DAY FOUR

*"Let the high praises of God be in their mouth, and a twoedged
sword in their hand; To execute vengeance upon the heathen,
and punishments upon the people; To bind their kings with
chains, and their nobles with fetters of iron; To execute upon
them the judgement written: this honour have all his saints.
Praise ye the LORD."*
Psalm 149:6-9 KJV

We have an enemy. There—I said it. Many people do not
want to hear about him. Many folks refuse to talk about him
for fear that they are glorifying him. Let me tell you; he is not
to be glorified, but how can we overcome an enemy that we
know nothing about?

Lucifer, satan, the devil. He was once a glorious being.
Ezekiel 28 describes him as "the model of perfection, full of
wisdom and exquisite in beauty." It goes on to tell of how he
was "adorned with every precious stone." What a beautiful
creature!

Many theologians believe that Lucifer was Heaven's
"worship leader." The said passage says that he was created
with tabrets and pipes, which are described as musical
instruments in several other places in scripture. Can you

imagine the music pouring out of this most splendid being even as he breathed each breath? This description of him is truly magnificent! But over time Lucifer began to behold his own magnificence instead of beholding the One Who is greater and more magnificent than any other—even the beautiful worship leader of Heaven.

And so, Lucifer was cast out of Heaven. His heavenly music ceased. His being fell silent of the marvelous music that it once created. Not only did Lucifer fall from Heaven, but he took one third with him in the fall. So, what was to happen? The thought of the beautiful worship coming forth from Lucifer coming to a halt seems devastating; but God already had a plan in place.

Fast forward to the present. Jesus has won the victory, the veil separating us from God's Presence has been torn, and now we have opportunity to lift music in praise and worship to our Father. And Lucifer? Well, he has other plans.

We are the ones that God has redeemed to himself. We are the ones that the Father sacrificed His Son for. We are the ones able to worship before the Lord now. God didn't send His Son for Lucifer. God didn't redeem Lucifer. He did that for us— His sons and daughters, created in His image. He did this for us and, frankly, the devil is jealous.

In his great jealousy and hatred toward us he tries to trip us up. He tries to keep us from fulfilling our God-given potential. He comes at us in many ways in an attempt to keep us from lifting our voice to the God he tried to exalt himself above. Yes, the enemy hates us. So, what do we do about this? How do we overcome our enemy?

Psalm 149 says with the *high praises of God in our mouths and a two-edged sword in our hand* the enemy king is *bound with chains and his nobles with fetters of iron.*

The first thing we need to do is keep the high praises of God in our mouths. When we walk around praising God all day it makes it difficult to allow our current situation to defeat our mindset. Whenever you feel the devil attacking you just begin to lift up the Name of the Lord! Whether you're at work, at home, in the car—wherever—you can give God praise and no matter where you are or what time of day He is able to hear you. Psalm 116 says that God bends down to listen to us. The Lord hears our voice! You don't have to wait until a certain time or place. Give God praise anywhere and everywhere; He will hear you!

The second part of this passage says that we should have a two-edged sword in our hand. Hebrews 4:12 says that the Word of God is alive, active and sharper than any *two-edged sword*. We defeat the enemy with praise AND with the Word.

When we combine the power of the Word along with the praise of our mouths it is an unstoppable force. The word of God never returns void and it always goes forth accomplishing what God wills.

The next time the devil tries to trip you up, put him back in his place by giving praise to your God straight from the Word! A great place to find some scriptures to use in praise and worship is the Book of Psalms. I often turn to the Psalms whenever I am facing something—or even when I'm not.

It is always a good time to praise God!

Precious Father, Your Name is great and greatly to be praised! May Your praises ever be on my lips! I give thanks to You God! Your unfailing love endures forever!

DAY FIVE

"And so, dear brothers and sisters, I plead with you to give your bodies to God because of all he has done for you. Let them be a living sacrifice—the kind he will find acceptable. This is truly the way to worship him"
Romans 12:1 NLT

Our waitress brought our food to the table where we were sitting. I noticed my wife, Haley, eyeing my plate. "I wish I would have gotten that! That looks really good!" Just then I felt the Holy Spirit speak to my heart. *Give her your plate.* I had a big decision to make. Should I give her the plate of food that I ordered and wanted so badly or just ignore God speaking to me? *Give her your plate.* Finally, acting quickly before I could change my mind, I grabbed her plate from her setting and replaced it with mine.

Although this seems like a small, silly incident, God showed me something about that day. Giving my plate to Haley was an actual act of worship. Even though it seemed small—small or not—it was a sacrifice! I made a sacrifice to obey God's direction to me.

Our days are made up of these kinds of moments. How often do you act on what God is telling you to do? Even when you are at the grocery store for instance. You see that the very front space in the parking lot is available and start towards it when suddenly you see an elderly woman heading toward the same spot. How do you react? Do you back off and allow her to have it—or do you speed up so that you can get pulled in before she gets it?

When you are in a hurry and realized that you no longer want a certain item, what do you do? Do you walk it back to its appropriate shelf and restock it—or simply lay it down on the shelf nearest to you? You are finally exiting the store. You take your groceries and load them into the trunk of your car and look down at your empty cart. Do you take the cart and put it away in one of the cart returns or merely leave it sitting in the parking spot beside you?

You may be wondering—*what does this have to do with worship? Isn't worship the slow songs we sing on Sunday mornings?* No, my friend, that is not what worship is.

Although music helps us to express love toward the Father, it is not worship in and of itself.

Romans 12:1 tells us that the way to truly worship God is to be a *living sacrifice*. It tells us that we should give our *bodies to Him because of what He has done for us.* How can we be a living sacrifice?

One way is doing what we know is right. Just like when I gave my food to my wife. I knew that God was telling me to give it to her and I nearly missed the opportunity. Wouldn't it had been a pity to have missed out on an act of worship and missed out on blessing my wife because of a certain meal? The sad thing is that people often miss out on acts of sacrifice to God and don't even realize the chances to worship passed them by.

Have you ever heard that still small voice tell you something like this: *Leave that last donut for your co-worker, he's having a rough week?* What do you do in these moments? Do you let the opportunity pass you by?

What I am trying to stress is that whenever we sacrifice our own wants, needs, and desires for others, we are *truly* worshiping God. Whenever we give in to our own wants and put them ahead of what God says, we are acting out the opposite of worship; we are acting in rebellion.

Sometimes we are looking for something grandiose and think that only the colossal things are from God—but God wants us to worship Him with every part of ourselves. From our song to our parking spot!

When we truly live a life of sacrifice in worship, we do our best to honor God in all aspects of our lives. That is when we become *a living sacrifice* and God will find our worship *pleasing and acceptable.*

Father, help me to live my life fully for you. Help me to be a living sacrifice that you find acceptable in Your sight! Help me not get so focused on the big things that I miss Your things. Whether great or small I choose to live a life of worship to You!
In Jesus' Name!

DAY SIX

*"It came even to pass, as the trumpeters and singers were as
one, to make one sound to be heard in praising and thanking
the LORD; and when they lifted up their voice with the trumpets
and cymbals and instruments of musick, and praised the LORD,
saying, For he is good; for his mercy endureth for ever: that
then the house was filled with a cloud, even the house of the
LORD; So that the priests could not stand to minister by reason
of the cloud: for the glory of the LORD had filled the house of
God."*
2 Chronicles 5:13-14 KJV

Have you ever shown up at church and just gone through the
motions? After a long, hard week behind you it can be easy to
just show up—and that's it. *I just want to sit back and enjoy
the service.* That is okay but just like anything else; you are
going to get out what you put in. If you plant a tomato seed,
you don't expect to get an apple tree.

Maybe you have been in a service and in walks someone you
have been harboring anger and resentment towards. You stand,
hands in your pockets during praise and worship and rehearse
over and over the things that you would like to say to him; but
this is church so maybe you will wait until Monday to unload
on him.

We are all human and have all had hard times, but when it comes to lifting the Name of the Lord we must realize that how we are feeling has no hold on Who God Is. He is the same whether we are in a good mood or in a bad mood. He is still faithful whether we are or not. He is still worthy. He never changes.

If we could all come together as a body with one intention— to praise and worship God—we too could see the glory of God, just as the priests did in 2 Chronicles 5! But so many times we come to church and never unify with other believers. I have experienced services where I could sense people whom, out of their own stubbornness, refused to press in and grieved the Holy Spirit. I, too, have been one of those people.

I remember a revival service years ago when I was leading worship. I was a fairly new Christ Follower and the revival was really starting to ignite. There were young people coming and getting saved, then going back to school and bringing their friends the next night. It was awesome! But there was a problem; I had been slightly offended by something the evangelist had said to me before one of the services and hadn't let go of it.

I stood to lead worship that night but all I could focus on was the anger that was welling up inside me. Needless to say, I staggered through the set. The presence of God that we had so evidenced the prior nights was not so evident anymore.

I sat through the message, refusing to acknowledge the evangelist during his message, and felt darkness clouding my heart. I finally sensed the Holy Spirit tell me that I was hindering Him and grieving Him by my thoughts and actions. With His help I was able to push through that junk and forgive the evangelist for what he had done. The crazy thing is I cannot even remember the thing that offended me so much. But I do remember the horrible feeling that I had when I was refusing to be unified with the other members of the body of Christ.

Psalm 33 speaks of unity. It says that unity is *good and pleasant*. It also says that *unity* is the place the Lord *commanded the blessing, even life for evermore!* You want to see God's blessings? Be unified! You want to experience the glory of God? Be unified!

2 Chronicles 5 says that the singers and trumpeters came together and lifted their voices as ONE. Then the glory of the Lord came in such a powerful way that the priests were unable to fulfill their duties. I don't know about you but I long to just sit and linger in the Presence of God. No pretense, just His Presence. Unity is the way to get there!

The next time you come together with your church family remember that we are a body and should be unified as one. When we do, the Presence of our God will arrive, and we will experience the glory that comes from it.

Father, help us to lift our voices to you as one! May we be unified together! May we sing our songs of praise and worship unto You and You alone. May we not be distracted by division but come together as a healthy body, functioning in tandem with one another. May we have one mind fixed completely on You. Show us Your Glory Lord!
In Jesus' Name!

DAY SEVEN

"Yet you are holy, enthroned on the praises of Israel."
Psalm 22:3 NLT

I love Psalm 22:3! It tells us that God is *enthroned* on the praises of His people! Isn't that exciting? To know that our God is enthroned on our praises is an incredible revelation to behold!

The definition of the word *enthroned* according to Merriam-Webster is: 1 a: to seat in a place associated with a position of authority or influence b: to seat ceremonially on a throne 2:to assign supreme virtue or value to: EXALT.

You see, when we praise God we are creating a throne, a place of authority in our lives for Him to be seated upon. We are creating a place in our lives that shows He has the influence in our lives, not ourselves. When He is seated upon our praises we are exalting Him by giving Him supreme virtue and value.

The Amplified Bible Classic Edition translates the verse as, *But You are holy, O You Who dwell in (the holy place where) the praises of Israel (are offered).* How incredible! We never have to wonder when or where God is going to show up because we already know.

Although, as followers of Christ, we know that God is always with us, we often long for His tangible Presence. We seek out His manifest Presence and go hard after it. But we need to keep one thing in mind—God is enthroned on our *praise!* He *dwells* in our *praise!* Basically, He lives there.

Our praise is where He can be found when we have been facing something that has kept us up all night praying, feeling as though our prayers were going no higher than the ceiling. Our praise is where He can be found when we are facing an illness and can't seem to find the peace we need. Our praise is where He can be found when we have just gotten laid off from our jobs and don't know which way to turn. Our praise is where He may be found when our child has made some bad choices and nothing we say to them seems to make them realize the error of their ways. He is in our praise!

And where else would He be? When Paul and Silas were locked in prison when were they set free? They were set free when they began to give God praise! What set into motion the enemy armies defeating themselves when Jehoshaphat's kingdom was facing peril? It happened when they began giving God praise! Just imagine what could happen in our lives if we would just begin to build God a throne on our praises for Him to dwell on!

The next time you are longing for God's Presence just remember where His dwelling place is: on the throne of your praise!

Oh God of Heaven and earth, I exalt You today! I give you praise! May You be enthroned upon my praise today and dwell there, for I long for You!

DAY EIGHT

"And so the Lord says, 'These people say they are mine. They honor me with their lips, but their hearts are far from me. And their worship of me is nothing but man-made rules learned by rote.'"
Isaiah 29:13 NLT

Have you ever done something out of mere habit? Maybe you have traveled the same route to work for many years. You realize one morning that you are sitting in the parking lot with no recollection of how you ended up there.

Have you ever had a routine down to such a fine art that if one little part of the routine is skipped or left out it throws you off completely? Maybe, for example, you get up every morning and brush your teeth then take your shower; but for one reason or another you get up and shower first and then are left wondering, *did I brush my teeth yet?*

Most of us can relate to these examples. We humans have the tendency to become creatures of habit. We fall into a certain pattern of doing things and then continue doing those same things over and over. These are not always bad things. It can certainly help us to accomplish the routine events of our day and keep us from leaving anything off of our list. But many times, this habitual pattern of doing things can run over into our spiritual lives and that is not a good thing.

God says in Isaiah, *They honor me with their lips, but their hearts are far from me.* God is not interested in lip service. He is the one Who knows our hearts. He knows our thoughts. He knows what is sincere and what isn't; but we often end up doing things routinely. We may not even realize it! The song of worship coming out of our lips may merely be the sound of noise to God's Ear. So how do we come to know whether our worship is sincere or not?

David, in Psalm 139:23-24, asked of the Lord, *Search me, O God, and know my heart; test me and know my anxious thoughts. Point out anything in me that offends you, and lead me along the path of everlasting life.*

If we ask of God to search our hearts and reveal the hidden things to us, He is good on His Word to carry it out! The Holy Spirit will continually search our hearts, shining a light on anything that has no place there. It is our responsibility to work with Him to remove that thing!

What is your heart and mind focused on when you come before the Lord? Are you completely focused upon God and His excellent ways—or are you distracted by the rigors of life? If the latter is more common for you then take a step back and allow God to examine your heart.

I am not saying that you should ever give up pressing in towards God's Presence. By all means! Keep pressing! But should you find yourself as one who's words are praiseworthy, but heart is distant from the Lord then it is time for a readjustment! God is not one who is fond of being lukewarm.

As a singer I am often on the search for my room temperature water. It is not good to drink cold water because it causes the muscles around the vocal cords to become stiff and tense. On the other hand, hot drinks may loosen the muscles but could harm the throat. I always try to keep my lukewarm water nearby. Unlike me, Jesus doesn't look for those who are lukewarm. He doesn't want room temperature. He wants someone who is on fire!

If you feel that your worship has been lacking recently and that your whole heart isn't in it then it is time for an overhaul! Ask the Holy Spirit to reveal the cause and to help you fix it!

Maybe you are just going through the motions and not giving any thought to the praise and worship you are offering up to God. It is time to come alive again! Allow the coals of your heart to be stoked by the Holy Spirit of God!

Holy Spirit, search my heart! If my worship has been stagnant then awaken me and help me to become one who's heart is fully after God! Ignite my desire for God once again!
In Jesus' Name!

DAY NINE

"But ye are a chosen generation, a royal priesthood, an holy nation, a peculiar people; that ye should shew forth the praises of him who hath called you out of darkness into his marvelous light:"
1 Peter 2:9 KJV

I believe that God is currently revealing more and more to us about the power that comes when His Name is exalted! We already touched on this in an earlier devotion, but it is necessary for us to return once again and explore the miraculous power that occurs when we praise and worship our King.

1 Peter 2:9 calls us believers a *royal priesthood*. This scripture is one that has been often quoted by evangelists and preachers, but I want to zero in on that one statement: we are a *royal priesthood.*

To fully understand what this scripture is telling us we must first take a look at what those two words mean. Let's begin with the word "royal."

Merriam-Webster defines royal – 1 a : of kingly ancestry b : of, relating to, or subject to the crown c : being in the crown's service 2 a : suitable for royalty : MAGNIFICENT b : requiring no exertion : EASY 3 a : of superior size, magnitude, or quality.

Priesthood is defined as: one authorized to perform the sacred rites of a religion especially as a mediatory agent between humans and God.

When we break it down we can clearly see that we, as a royal priesthood, are ones who have been given authority to minister before the Lord! As royal priests, we have an opportunity to come boldly before the throne of God!

We become people who have authority and are able to minister unto the Lord and see the miraculous take place in His Presence! I don't know about you but that makes me excited!

When we take our place as the authoritative servant we make room for the manifest Presence of God to settle and wherever the Presence of the Lord Is there is freedom! Freedom for the sick! Freedom for the hopeless! Freedom for those who are bound!

Being a "Servant with Authority" may sound like a contradiction but I assure you that you must be both if you are to be a *royal priest*. You see, we have been given authority— and yet we have no authority apart from God's Authority. He is the reason we have the authority to begin with. If we aren't standing on the authority of Jesus, then we have none to stand on.

At the same time, we become His servants when we begin to minister unto Him. We begin to serve Him and it is then that we are exalted.

Once we find that balance between being a *royal subject* and a *priest* we will see the mighty, wonder-working power of God on display for all to see! But we must find the balance between the two!

When we lean too far to the authoritative side we are in danger of becoming puffed up, as well as being unmerciful and unloving, in our actions toward others.

When we go too far the other way our servant heart can quickly become a weak and wimpy heart. We take the chance of becoming burnt out and turning from the way we should go.

But when we get our lives in balance and truly become a *royal priesthood* we set ourselves up to see the mighty power of God revealed to us and others!

Father, thank you for making me a royal priest! Oh God who has called me out of darkness into Your marvelous light; help me to show forth Your praises forever!

DAY TEN

*"And David danced before the LORD with all his might,
wearing a priestly garment."*
2 Samuel 6:14 NLT

David's wife, Michal stared out of the window. Her heart
was filled with disgust. *How undignified! What a chaotic
display! The king is acting so foolishly! Did his priestly
garment just fall to the ground amid this child-like dancing?*
Yes, Michal's heart was filled with contempt toward her
husband.

The Ark of God's Covenant had just made its triumphant
return to Jerusalem; though it wasn't without cost. David's
original plan was to place the ark upon a cart and bring it back
to the city. It was loaded onto the man-made structure and
began its progression toward Jerusalem. Abinadab's sons,
Ahio and Uzzah were tasked with the duty of walking along
with the ark as the oxen pulled it along. When the oxen
stumbled Uzzah reached out his hand to steady the ark and was
struck dead.

David's heart was filled with anger toward God. *How could
God do this? After all, weren't we trying to honor the LORD?*
What David had failed to realize was that God had already

given certain rules and regulations concerning the ark. It was to be *carried upon the shoulders of the priests.*

One of the first revelations we can glean from this story is that, as *royal priests* we have the responsibility of carrying the Presence of the Lord upon our shoulders. We often try to create a place for God in our own means and in our own strength. Although it may not be a cart made of wood—we sometimes try to fit God into a certain program. At times we try to recreate a service based on what worked last week instead of truly seeking God and finding out what His plan is. We must remember that God's Way is higher than our way. If we are to carry the Presence of the Lord on our shoulders as priests of God, we must be willing to take up our cross and move forward instead of trying to take the easy way. The "way of the cart" will only lead us to spiritual death.

Like David, when our plans fail we often become angry at God. *But this was done with the best of intentions!* Good intentions do not always equal God's intentions. We must be like David and come against those wrong feelings. We must re-group and seek what God would have us to do—then do it!

Finally, when the time comes for God's Presence to enter in we must be willing to get over ourselves and respond with joy! David danced with all his might before the Presence of God! Are you willing to respond to Him? Responding will also cost you something.

We must be willing to become as a child. We must be willing to let go of any pride that we may be harboring. We must be willing to humble ourselves before the Lord. We cannot be preoccupied with what other people think of us. We must also refuse to care what we even think of ourselves! And then there is Michal.

When David returned home to bless his family Michal was there waiting for him. She scolded him. She mocked him. She even went so far as to demean him about his actions before the maidservants. But David responded to Michal with these words, "I was dancing before the LORD, who chose me above your father and all his family! He appointed me as the leader of Israel, the people of the LORD, so I celebrate before the LORD. Yes, and I am willing to look even more foolish than this, even to be humiliated in my own eyes! But those servant girls you mentioned will indeed think that I am distinguished!" David was willing to allow himself to look like a fool for God's glory. Are you? Michal wasn't so willing. 2 Samuel 6:23 says, *So Michal, the daughter of Saul, remained childless throughout her entire life.* Nothing good was ever birthed from her life.

This is our final lesson; when we refuse to humble ourselves before the Lord and call His anointed as foolishness we will never birth anything good. I don't know about you, but I want God to be glorified in my life—even if I must become "undignified" to do so.

God of all creation, I humble myself before You! Help me to see your plan and be responsive to it! May I give you praise all my days even if it costs me my reputation in doing so! You are my God! You define me!

DAY ELEVEN

*"My heart has heard you say, 'Come and talk with me.' And
my heart responds, 'LORD, I am coming.'"*
Psalm 27:8 NLT

Isn't it amazing that the God of all mankind would ask us to
come talk with Him? The very God Who hung the stars in the
sky, Who separated the day from the night, Who caused the
universe to fall into orbit, Who created not only vastness but
also the smallest cells, molecules, etc., is asking us to come
talk with Him! This should excite us greatly! And what
should our reaction be when we come before Him? To
worship Him!

When we come before the Lord and experience His majestic
Presence how else could we respond? When Isaiah came
before Him he was overcome! When John beheld the throne of
God He was awestruck with the glory of the Lord! When the
manifest Presence of God fell in the temple the priests were

unable to continue their sacrificial work. After Jesus was resurrected and visited the disciples, even though some were in disbelief, they yet fell down and worshiped the Risen King. Our God is an overwhelming God!

Overwhelming grace. Overwhelming love. Overwhelming wisdom. Overwhelming power. With such an overwhelming God our reaction should always be to bow before Him and worship the One Who sits on the throne, the Eternal King!

What is your response when God beckons you to come talk with Him? Do you respond as the psalmist and cry out, "Lord, I am coming" or do you even realize that He *is* calling you to come unto Him?

To know that our God speaks to us we must realize that our God does indeed speak to us! We must be "tuned-in", so to speak. We must be able to distinguish His Voice from the other voices that present themselves to us—including our own.

So how do we come to recognize God's Voice? For starters, we must know His Word. We must understand His Nature. We must know that at times our flesh and/or the enemy will try to speak to us and we must know immediately that there are certain things that God will never ask us to do. Ever hear of the Ten Commandments? You can bet that God will never ask you to do anything that goes against those; making that a good place to start.

Also, God will never tell us negative things. Even when He shines a light on certain areas of our life that we need to clean up He will always do so in the form of conviction and not through condemnation. The Word says that there is now therefore NO condemnation for those who are in Christ Jesus. When God speaks we may stand in awe, but He will never bring you a word through a spirit of fear!

Another way we come to know and recognize the Voice of our Lord is through prayer. You know, talking with God. You talk a little and then He talks back to you. The verse in Psalm 27 says that God is asking us to talk *with Him* not *at Him*. Just as it isn't much fun to be with someone who does all the talking and doesn't allow anyone else to speak, we must give God a chance to speak, as well. He *is* God, after all!

Finally, a third way that we can come to recognize and hear the Voice of God is through worship. This is a time when we are before Him and His Glory shines down on us, changing us. We become a reflection of His Brilliance more and more. The more time we spend in His Presence the more we will become like Him! When we become more like Him the more we will recognize His Voice, His Nature, and His Ways.

God is calling you to come talk with Him today. How will you respond?

God, I know that You are calling me to come before You and talk with You! Lord, I am coming!

DAY TWELVE

"One thing have I desired of the LORD, that will I seek after;
that I may dwell in the house of the LORD all the days of my
life, to behold the beauty of the LORD, and to inquire in his
temple."
Psalm 27:4 KJV

W hen you dig deep and examine yourself what is the one thing you desire above all else? Money? Fame? Family? Career? David had a desire.

In years past I also had a desire. Before I was saved (and for awhile after) I had a lust for fame, fortune, and worldly success. I had grown up very poor but one day I realized that I had a voice and was able to sing.

I practiced and practiced and practiced some more. Finally, an opportunity opened for me and I was able to sing before an audience for the first time. I stood up before a crowd at our local Country Dance Club (yes, this was at the height of the Country Music Line Dance craze) and belted out a tune. I had no band, so I stood there and sang acapella. As I finished the room burst into applause. The men hooped and hollered, and the women were wiping tears from their eyes. I was so taken back that I felt like I was walking three feet above the floor. That is the place when and where a bad seed was planted.

I felt accepted in a way that I had never felt before. I wasn't one of the 'cool kids' and not many of the students in my class at school wanted to hang around me. When I received such applause, I went on a quest to replicate that experience.

After awhile the sensation of having 100 or so people applauding for me lost its savor. I wanted more. I quickly decided that I was going to be rich and famous. It all started out of a desire to be loved. I developed a perverted view of what love really was. Soon my one true desire above everything else was to become the most famous singer in the world!

Fast forward several years later. I heard the gospel and it struck me deeply. I was saved, and Jesus was now my Savior. God began to shine a light on certain things in my life and He revealed to me that my one true desire for fame was wrong. God began working in me. He took my heart of stone and gave me a heart of flesh. I knew that to move forward in Him and to step into the calling He had placed on my life I had to let go of the lust for fame and take hold of Him.

I can tell you today after experiencing the Presence of the Lord nothing can compare with Him! Fame and fortune are of no value when compared to God's glory! It is easy to understand why David desired it above all else!

I once sang out of an effort to be loved. Now I know that I am loved—therefore I sing! Also, I now know that we cannot worship something that is not our one true desire.

What do you desire? If you desire something other than God, know that the more time you spend with Him the more you will desire Him. Philippians 2:13 says that "God is working in you, giving you the desire and power to do what pleases Him."

If you keep allowing God to work in you, He will become your desire. When we humble ourselves before Him and worship Him in spirit and truth, He will flood our lives with His love and power. We *will* behold the beauty of His Splendor! He *will* become the desire of our hearts!

Almighty God, may you be our one true desire! If you are not, then please help us Holy Spirit. Help us to desire God more and more. We humble ourselves before You! Help us to understand your awesome majesty, in Jesus' Name.

DAY THIRTEEN

"After consulting the people, the king appointed singers to walk ahead of the army, singing to the LORD and praising him for his holy splendor. This is what they sang: 'Give thanks to the LORD; his faithful love endures forever!' At the very moment they began to sing and give praise, the LORD caused the armies of Ammon, Moab, and Mount Seir to start fighting among themselves. The armies of Moab and Ammon turned against their allies from Mount Seir and killed everyone of them. After they destroyed the army of Seir, they began attacking each other. So when the army of Judah arrived at the lookout point in the wilderness, all they saw were dead bodies lying on the ground as far as they could see. Not a single one of the enemy had escaped."
2 Chronicles 20:21—24 NLT

Praise and worship are powerful tools. They are also very important in our spiritual walk. We were created to worship God. It is also the very thing that we will be doing in Heaven. As I said in earlier devotions, the Book of Revelation gives us a glimpse into the activities of Heaven and guess what? We will be worshiping!

Today I want to share with you the power that comes from worshiping the Almighty God.

Jehoshaphat was terrified by the news he had just received. Word came to him that the combined armies of the Ammonites, Moabites, and Meunites were marching against Judah. He ordered that everyone in Judah would begin fasting. The people fasted and began seeking the Lord.

Jehoshaphat stood before the people and they prayed corporately. When finished on of the men of Judah spoke up as the Holy Spirit descended upon him. He said, "Do not be afraid! Don't be discouraged by this mighty army, for the battle is not yours, but God's."

The day came when it was time to march forward. Before he sent the army off, Jehoshaphat gave a rather strange order. He told the singers to march *ahead* of the army. They were to praise God in song, singing *Give thanks to the LORD; his faithful love endures forever!*

An amazing thing happened that day. As the worship leaders sang out praises unto God, the enemy armies defeated each other. Without having to lift a finger in (physical) battle the victory had been won. Not only that but Judah collected all the plunder from their defeated enemies!

There are several lessons that we can learn from this; the first of these is that when we lift up the Name of God our enemy is defeated! Praise and worship are powerful weapons in the spiritual realm!

We can also summarize that:

1. Judah stopped looking at their problem and started looking at their God! Whenever you face something that is causing you trouble, take your eyes off the problem and look at your God!
2. They remembered what God had already done for them. Has God ever done anything good for you? Bring it back to your mind and remember how faithful He has been to you in times past!

3. They stopped looking at themselves and fixed their eyes on God! Sometimes we think that we must do God's job for Him. That is never a good idea. Step back and allow God to be your strength!
4. They put the praise and worship of God first. In the natural this sounds crazy, but this is why the battle was won! They received the victory when the Name of the Lord was lifted up!

The effects of their worship was felt throughout the land! The same effects that Judah felt are also available to you today when you praise and worship God!

A. Their song of praise caused confusion in the enemy camp. In the flesh this doesn't make logical sense—to praise and worship in the midst of a battle—but in the spiritual world it is a mighty weapon!
B. The enemy was defeated. Worship causes the forces of darkness to become the instrument of its own destruction.
C. The Israelites received the plunder from the enemy's camp. Maybe Satan has stolen things from you. Has he stolen your joy? Your hope? Your peace? It is time to lift up the Name of the Lord and take back what Satan has tried to steal.
D. The more time you spend worshiping God the more you will come to know Him. You will desire to become more and more like Him and He will empower you to do so.
E. The surrounding kingdoms heard what God had done. When you begin to worship God and witness His Power on display, word will spread, and others will want to know more about the One you are serving! They will learn of Jesus Christ and how your life has been touched by the One True Living God!

I want you to know today that God rewards those who diligently seek Him. One of the ways we seek Him is through praise and worship. Are you facing a problem today? Praise

Him! Have you lost your joy? Praise Him! Have you lost your peace? Praise Him! Have you lost hope? Praise Him! No matter what you are facing today, God is still God! He is still holy! He is still worthy! Praise Him!

Our Most Holy God, You are good! Your faithful love endures forever!

DAY FOURTEEN

*"When a certain immoral woman from that city heard he was
eating there, she brought a beautiful alabaster jar filled with
expensive perfume. The she knelt behind him at his feet
weeping. Her tears fell on his feet, and she wiped them off with
her hair. Then she kept on kissing his feet and putting perfume
on them."*
Luke 7:37-38 NLT

She had done many wrong things in her life. You can sense
from the passage that her heart was full of shame. To add
insult to injury, the Pharisees looked down on her for being
such an "immoral woman." The Word gives us a peak into the
thoughts of the Pharisee whose house Jesus was visiting.
   *If this man were a prophet, he would know what kind of
woman is touching him. She's a sinner!* Now, before we begin
judging the Pharisee let us stop for a minute and examine our

own hearts. Would we have thought the same thoughts? Especially given the culture and place in history that this took place—would we have been more like the "immoral woman" or would we have been more like the Pharisee? If we immediately express judgement against the Pharisee, then we *become* the Pharisee!

What were Jesus' thoughts about this? Was He shocked at this woman's actions? Thankfully, scripture let's us know exactly what Jesus thought about it all.

Jesus was able to know the thoughts of the Pharisee and answered him accordingly; *Simon, I have something to say to you. A man loaned money to two people—500 pieces of silver to one and 50 pieces to the other. But neither of them could repay him, so he kindly forgave them both, canceling their debts. Who do you suppose loved him more after that?*

Simon answered, "I suppose the one for whom he canceled the larger debt."

Jesus then responded, "That's right. Look at this woman kneeling here. When I entered your home, you didn't offer me water to wash the dust from my feet, but she has washed them with her tears and wiped them with her hair. You didn't greet me with a kiss, but from the time I first came in, she has not stopped kissing my feet. You neglected the courtesy of olive oil to anoint my head, but she has anointed my feet with rare perfume. I tell you, her sins—and they are many—have been forgiven, so she has shown me much love. But a person who is forgiven little shows only little love." Then Jesus said to the woman, "Your sins are forgiven. Your faith has saved you; go in peace."

The good news is this—no matter if you are the weeping woman or the judging Pharisee—there is salvation found in Jesus Christ for all of us!

You may be asking yourself what any of this has to do with worship. I tell you, this has *everything* to do with worship!

The woman brought what she had to the feet of Jesus. Not only her box full of expensive perfume, but also her tears, guilt, shame, etc. and left them at Jesus' feet. Then she knelt low before Him. In one act of humility and surrender she left her tears mixed with the expensive perfume at His feet and walked away forgiven!

We are imperfect beings. Although we are being renewed day by day into the likeness of Jesus, we will never reach protection on this temporal side of eternity. Therefore, we can bring our imperfections to Jesus—but we must not forget to bring the best that we have, *all* of us, to His feet. We must be willing to bow before God in surrender to Him. We must come to the place where we pour ourselves out before Him in worship. When we do this, He will fill us up with more of Him! There is nothing to lose here other than our tears and the best *we've* got—but our best is nothing compared to *His* best!

So, go before Him today! Pour it all out before Him! Your best *and* your worst and allow Him to take it off of you and He will give you His best!

My Precious Savior, I pour myself out before you today. I humbly bow before Your Majesty in surrender to You! Here I am! I worship Your holy Name Jesus! Make me more and more like You!

DAY FIFTEEN

*"Around midnight Paul and Silas were praying and singing
hymns to God, and the other prisoners were listening.
Suddenly there was a massive earthquake, and the prison was
shaken to its foundations. All the doors immediately flew open,
and the chains of every prisoner fell off!"*
Acts 16:25-26 NLT

Paul and Silas were doing what God had called them to do
and what was the result? They were thrown into prison!

There may be times when we are truly fulfilling the call that
God has placed upon us that we find ourselves bound by
certain things. We may from time to time find ourselves in
situations that are less than desired. How will we handle
ourselves during these times?

Have you seen and felt the midnight darkness surrounding
you? God never promised that we would never face the
night—but He did promise to be there with us, shining His
light around us illuminating the darkness.

Maybe you are currently bound by something. You might find yourself wondering, *How am I going to overcome this?* Maybe the door of opportunity that you have been waiting for seems to have slammed shut on you. Have you heard the "clank of the door and the turn of the key?"

Paul and Silas literally heard that sound. Their response is a good lesson on what to do in those times when we have become bound and imprisoned. What did they do?

Acts 16 tells us that in that midnight hour the two were *praying and singing hymns to God!* What a reaction! When we find ourselves in desperate situations our first reaction should always be to turn to God! Amazing things happen when we do!

The Word tells us that even before the great earthquake *the other prisoners were listening!* How we handle ourselves during trying times is important because others are watching you. When we whine and complain, others will see and wonder how you, as a follower of Christ, are any different than they are; but when we give God praise in good times *and* bad times others will take notice.

Paul and Silas had a right attitude and the Bible says that *suddenly* there was a massive earthquake! God will begin to shake up your life when you react in a right way. When you refuse to sing the blues and instead sing His praise, God will rock your world—and the world of those around you!

Next, the doors of the prison flew open and the chains of *every* prisoner fell off! When we set our minds to praise God our prison doors will open, and our chains of bondage will be broken. Even beyond that; those who are imprisoned around us will be set free from the testimony of the example you have placed before them!

Later in this passage we learn that the jailer, through this chain of events, heard the gospel and he, along with his entire household, was saved! God is able to do above and beyond anything we can ask or think. He is able to use your faithfulness as a testament of Who He is. When we handle ourselves in a way that gives glory to God, we will see others come to know Him!

Let's give God praise in *every* situation! When we do we will find that He will release us from our bondage and will set others free, also! When we live a life of praise we will see those around us become Christ Followers—even those we thought were meant to be an instrument to defeat us!

Praise God today, no matter what your situation may be!

Praise the Lord! Praise to the One Who opens prison doors, breaks chains, and sets me free! May I always be an instrument of praise unto You!

DAY SIXTEEN

*"You have turned my mourning into joyful dancing. You have
taken away my clothes of mourning and clothed me with joy,
that I might sing praises to you and not be silent. O LORD my
God, I will give you thanks forever!"*
Psalm 30:11-12 NLT

What a wonderful God we serve! As the scripture says, He
gives us joyful dancing in place of mourning! He clothes us in
joy! I will say it again; what a wonderful God we serve!

Many people have a completely wrong vision of who God is.
They picture Him as seated upon a throne with a hammer in
His Hand, ready to pour His wrath upon them. In times past I,
also, viewed God in this manner.

Whenever I would mess up I would beg, cry, and plead with
God for mercy. I would start to feel better and then condemn
myself all over again. Sunday would come around and I would
be ready to praise and worship God with my brothers and
sisters until I would be reminded of how I treated my wife
badly the day before, or how I failed to give my children the
attention I should have given them, or how I hadn't spent
enough time with God in my prayer closet the week before. By
this time, I felt as though I had no right to come boldly before
His Throne. I would hold back in my guilt and let the
opportunity pass me by.

One day I was driving down the road feeling that old condemnation rising-up once again when I felt God speak to my heart. He said, *I love you and I am not sitting on the edge of my throne waiting for an opportunity to punish you. On the contrary, I am sitting on the edge of my throne waiting for an opportunity to bless you and spend time with you.* This statement was a Godsend (pun fully intended)!

I began to see that it wasn't God condemning me. The Bible tells us that there is *no condemnation* in Christ Jesus! But there is an enemy who accuses us of wrongdoing. I had been listening to the wrong voice all the time.

I am not saying that we shouldn't repent of our wrongs—we should! But Jesus paid the way for us and we can rest assured that once we repent we no longer need to punish ourselves for something that God chooses to forget!

Today I challenge you to forgive as God forgives! Forgive yourself! God is not waiting for an opportunity to banish you. He wants to bless you! Come boldly before Him and sing His praises as one who is forgiven and loved by God!

Father, thank you for the opportunity to come into Your Presence with no guilt, shame, or condemnation! Thank You Jesus for making a way for me! Holy Spirit, thank You for Your comfort, teaching, and power! Lead me to the throne of God!

DAY SEVENTEEN

"Sing a new song to the LORD! Let the whole earth sing to the LORD!"
Psalm 96:1 NLT

The Bible is full of exhortations that call out for the old to pass and for new things to come to life! New songs, new life, new hope, new name, new Heaven, new earth, new, new, new! Some try to equate being a Christian with being outdated, old, and bland; but the Word of Truth tells us a much different story!

God is calling us to move ahead and become new! We are serving the One Who makes *all things new!* How exciting is that? We are not to be put out to pasture and live a dull, boring life. We are meant to become new!

One of the areas that the Bible speaks of becoming new is in the area of our song. Now before we go on let me remind you of the fact that music is *not* worship but merely an instrument we use to express our love to God. It is also a vehicle that God uses to express His love toward us.

When we are saved and receive salvation we are called forward to sing our new song to the Lord. He has given us this precious new song through the blood of His Son, by the power of the Holy Spirit. This song is much more valuable than any other song ever written in the history of mankind! It is a song of worship to our king. You don't have to have a voice like Freddie Mercury or Whitney Houston. You don't have to have the songwriting skills of Diane Warren or Burt Bacharach. You must merely be open to the Holy Spirit in leading you to sing this song that He has given you. You only need to open your heart to the Lord in gratitude and humility in awe of the Lord.

Try singing your new song to Him. It doesn't have to be poetic. It doesn't have to rhyme. It must only be sincere. Sing of the things that He has brought you through. Sing of the ways He helps you from day to day. Sing of His awesome power, His love, and His mercy. Sing of the sacrifice that He made in order for you to be able to sing this new song.

Worshiping God should never be perceived as something boring or bland. It is a privilege to come before Him and bow down in reverence. The highest price which was ever paid for anything was paid by Jesus so that you could have this opportunity.

Our new song brings with it a new outlook! We can have hope for tomorrow because of the new thing that Christ did.

Sing a new song to the LORD! May all the earth sing Your praise!

DAY EIGHTEEN

"But King David replied to Araunah, "No, I insist on buying it for the full price. I will not take what is yours and give it to the LORD. I will not present burnt offerings that have cost me nothing!"
1 Chronicles 21:24 NLT

The angel of the LORD came to Gad telling him to instruct David to build an altar on the threshing floor of Araunah. David went to Araunah and asked to buy the threshing floor from him, but Araunah offered it to the king free-of-charge. David refused and insisted on paying for the land because he was unwilling to offer worship unto the Lord that had *cost him nothing.*

Before I proceed let me be very clear about something. Our salvation cost us nothing—and costed God everything. We cannot earn our salvation because it has already been earned for us by and through Jesus Christ. But, unlike salvation, true spiritual *worship* will cost us something.

There have been times in my life when I have felt God putting His Finger on something to get my attention. I have felt the promptings that if I would cooperate with the Holy Spirit in fixing the problem I would go into a deeper, more intimate relationship with my Creator.

You see, if we want to *truly* worship God it will indeed cost us something. It will cost us our pride. It will cost us our fear. It will cost us our selfish desires. It will cost us *something*.

I pray that we all come to the place where, regardless of cost, we would desire God more than anything else. Is there anything more valuable? Absolutely not! No matter what price we must pay to grow into a deeper relationship with the Lord, I can assure you that it is worth it!

Kathrine Kuhlman, when asked about what it would cost to have a ministry like she had, replied in her very dramatic way, "It costs everything…" Are you willing to pay the price?

Father allow us to come to the realization that You are more valuable than anything else. May we realize that whatever we must pay to worship You in spirit and truth—it is worth everything! Be glorified God.

DAY NINETEEN

*"May the nations praise you, O God. Yes, may all the nations
praise you. Let the whole world sing for joy, because you
govern the nations with justice and guide the people of the
whole world."*
Psalm 67:3-4 NLT

Last year I went on a mission trip to India. When we arrived,
everything seemed so strange to me. The buildings were
different. The food was different. The sounds and smells were
different. The language was different.

I was having quite a difficult time adjusting to our new
surroundings. I wasn't used to the spices used in the food and,
therefore, I was beginning to feel sick. Beyond that, I wasn't
used to being away from my wife and children and had a bad
case of homesickness. Another thing that I was missing was
Domino's Pizza. Oh, the will-power it took to overcome that!

Nonetheless I decided to hunker down and try to make the
best out of the trip. I believed that God had sent me there for a
reason and I knew that someone was going to learn something
from our visit there—whether it was them or me.

We visited a local church and began having meetings there.
The plan was that each of the four missionaries would speak at
the local church to a group of pastors, then the week would

culminate with an outdoor event (of which thousands attended).

When the day came for me to speak, I felt that God had called me to speak about the power of praise and worship. I was concerned that my "flow" would be compromised since I was using an interpreter.

As I stood to speak I was feeling very nervous. I was hoping that what I had to say would not get lost in translation. I opened my mouth and I experienced an anointing on me that I had never experienced before while preaching. The interpreter and I flowed together with ease. When God has a plan, He is the One Who carries it out!

At the end of the message I said, "praise Him!" As soon as I said those words, the people raised their hands in a holy roar! The power of God was so strong that all I could do was stand with my hands lifted toward Heaven, praising God with my lips. At that moment I felt a connection to the people of India that I had not felt prior.

You see, we are very different in many ways—but we are the same in the things that really matter. We are sons and daughters of the living God! When I raised my voice in praise, it intermingled with their voices and we were one and the same. All the things that separated us disappeared!

Praise not only connects us with God, but it can also connect us with the family of believers around the world! No matter where our location may be, we are to be of *one mind* and *one accord*. Our praise comes up before the throne of God. Every language, every nation. When we praise God, it tears down the walls that we have placed between "us and them" and we are revealed as *one body*.

Keep in mind that you are one voice in the mighty choir of God! What an honor it is to be a part of something greater than we are! May all the nations praise the Lord!

We join in with our family of believers around the world and offer you praise! Praise the Lord!

DAY TWENTY

"Draw near to God and He will draw near to you..."
James 4:8a. NKJV

When we come before God to worship Him, we are drawing near to Him. It is us acknowledging that He is God, therefore allowing us to come close to Him.

There are times in all our lives when God feels so close to us that we can tangibly feel Him near. There are also times when it may seem that God is nowhere near us. You know; those times when our praise, worship, and prayers don't seem to be going any higher than the ceiling. This can be very discouraging if we don't understand that what we feel isn't always the way things are.

The promises that are listed throughout God's Word are always true. Always. The truths that are in the Bible aren't dependent upon our feelings. If God says it in the good book, then you can rest assured that He means it; on our good days *and* our not-so-good days.

In James 4 God says that when we draw near to Him, He will in turn draw near to us! We can be sure in knowing that when we begin to move closer to God in worship that He is coming closer to us as well! Whether you 'feel it' or not, He is.

How exciting is it to know that the very God Who spoke the universe into existence, the Alpha and Omega, God Almighty is coming in close to you! God never fails to fulfill His Promises to you! Draw near to Him and He *will* draw near to you!

Today as you go about your day, make a conscious effort to draw nearer to Him. Make worshiping God a priority in your life today and every other day!

You wouldn't let an opportunity pass you by to spend time in the presence of your favorite celebrity or sports star, would you? How much more should we eagerly accept the invitation that has been given to us by the God of all creation?

Don't let this opportunity pass you by today. Draw near to God. Worship Him today. When you do you can be sure of the fact that He will be drawing nearer to you as well!

Lord, may we never take you for granted. Today I draw near to you and I know that as I do, You are drawing nearer to me!

DAY TWENTY-ONE

"There in front of the Tabernacle, Solomon went up to the bronze altar in the Lord's presence and sacrificed 1,000 burnt offerings on it. That night God appeared to Solomon and said, "What do you want? Ask, and I will give it to you!"
2 Chronicles 1:6-7 NLT

It is time for radical praise and worship! I am tired of the same-old, mundane song and dance! How about you? Wouldn't you like to go all out for God in your worship of Him? Solomon did.

Many times in scripture we see God speaking to His people, giving them direction on where to go, what to say, and what to do. We read that He often tells His people what He would like for them to do; but this particular passage in 2 Chronicles with Solomon and his offering unto the Lord is quite different. We see that after he presents his offering to the Lord, God asks what *he* wants God to do for him!

Let's backtrack a little. We see earlier in the passage that Solomon sacrificed *1,000* burnt offerings unto the Lord! 1,000! Can you imagine the look on the priest's faces when they saw Solomon coming with his 1,000 offerings?

The Bible says that when we delight ourselves in the Lord that He will give us the desires of our hearts. It is very clear from the abundance of his offering that Solomon was indeed delighting in the Lord; and God's response speaks volumes. "What do you want? Ask, and I will give it to you!"

Now, I am not promoting worshiping God so that you are able to get whatever you would like from Him. That is not worship—that is manipulation, and God will not be mocked. My point is this; when we truly worship God with all our hearts He rewards us for it. Not because we should have whatever we want but because He is good!

It is time that we get radical with our sacrifice of praise! Let's not withhold worship from Him because He is a great, faithful, and worthy God!

Lord, I could never worship You enough—but I won't let that stop me from worshiping you anyway! I will be extravagant in my praise to You!

DAY TWENTY-TWO

"Shout with joy to the LORD, all the earth! Worship the LORD
with gladness. Come before him, singing with joy.
Acknowledge that the LORD is God! He made us, we are his.
We are his people, the sheep of his pasture. Enter his gates
with thanksgiving; go into his courts with praise. Give thanks
to him and praise his name. For the LORD is good. His
unfailing love continues forever, and his faithfulness continues
to each generation."
Psalm 100 NLT

When the time comes to enter in to the Presence of the Lord,
what is your posture? We are to come before Him in honor
and respect; but we are also meant to share in the joy that
emanates from His Presence! We aren't meant to feel just a
little joy, we are meant to be filled with joy; so much that we
shout it out!

Psalm 100 teaches us that the pathway to the holy of holies,
or God's Presence, is through a pathway of joy and gladness!

We first enter His gates with thanksgiving. How thankful
are you? Begin to list all the blessings that God has given you.
I am sure that you will find that it is impossible to list *every*
single blessing that you have been given—and that doesn't
even count the times that He has blessed you without you even

knowing about it! Begin to thank Him! A thankful heart is the entryway (gate) into His Presence!

Next, the psalmist teaches us that we enter His courts with praise. One way of thinking of praise is to list the great works of God and call them out. Has He delivered you? Saved you? Healed you? Open your mouth and begin praising Him!

There have been times when I longed to feel close to God, but I couldn't seem to get through. It was during these times that I began to open my mouth and praise Him. Before long I felt the burden lift and I could feel myself drawing nearer and nearer to Him. Praise is powerful!

Today, before you go off to work, school, the grocery— wherever it is you may be heading off to—begin your day in His Presence. Enter His gates with thanksgiving and His courts with praise and let the joy of the Lord fill your heart and mind!

Thank You for the joy that is found in Your Presence! Today I choose to enter Your gates with thanksgiving and Your courts with praise!

DAY TWENTY-THREE

"For where two or three gather together because they are
mine, I am there among them."
Matthew 18:20 NLT

There have been many times while leading the congregation
in singing "The King Is Here" that I have closed my eyes and
envisioned Jesus walking up and down the aisles of the church.
I could sense Him being there in our midst! Then we would
get to the bridge and I felt like the king's subject proclaiming
excitedly from the rooftops, "The King is here! The King is
here! Hallelujah! God, You're here!" And He was, indeed!

I love what Jesus says in Matthew 18:20; He says, "where
two or three are gathered together in My Name, I will be there
in the midst." We know that God never lies. Whenever He
gives us His Word, He means it! If He says that He will be
there, then He will be there! Does that excite you? Doesn't
that make you long to be in the house of the Lord, gathered
together with your brothers and sisters in Christ?

Jesus gave us His Word, and we should always be aware that
when we gather together to honor Him—He *is* there!

Imagine that your favorite athlete/actor/musician, etc., were
going to be somewhere. Think about the excitement you
would feel for that. Think about the preparations you would
make if the President of the United States of America was
coming to spend time with you, one-on-one. How would you
show your admiration to such celebrities and dignitaries? How
much more should we show our admiration for the King who is
above every other king? How much more should we honor the
Name that is above every other name?

This week as you head off to church, remember Matthew 18:20. Remember that the One Who paid it all, the only One Who is worthy will be there, too!

The King is here! The King is here! Hallelujah! God, You're here!

DAY TWENTY-FOUR

"...the wise men went their way. And the star they had seen in the east guided them to Bethlehem. It went ahead of them and stopped over the place where the child was. When they saw the star, they were filled with joy! They entered the house and saw the child with his mother, Mary, and bowed down and worshiped him. Then they opened their treasure chests and gave him gifts of gold, frankincense, and myrrh."
Matthew 2:9-11 NLT

We have seen the scenario played out before us countless times before in media, art, and the like. You know the scene: Mary and Joseph standing over the peacefully sleeping baby Jesus as they are surrounded by a host of wild-stock, angels, a handful of shepherds, sometimes a little drummer boy, and three wise men with gifts-in-hand ready to be offered to the newborn child. It conjures up a very warm image leaving us feeling all "Christmas-y" inside.

The truth of the matter is much more dramatic. Here was the King above every other willingly allowing Himself to descend from His throne to be born in a barn and placed in a manger. There was also the matter of the earthly king who wanted nothing more than for the child to be killed. And what about those wise men with the small, perfectly wrapped and bowed Christmas gifts? What is *that* all about?

The real story is this: these wise men knew that they were witnessing the birth of their Savior. When they entered His Presence, they bowed low and worshiped Him. And then there is the matter of those gifts.

You see, those gifts weren't just the bible-times version of the cheap cologne you pick up at the local dollar store for the $5 office gift exchange. They were expensive and had great worth. The wise men brought their best to their King—and we should do the same!

Have you ever brought the equivalent of cheap cologne to offer unto the Lord? By the way, I am not talking about presenting Him with actual cologne. I am talking in spiritual terms here. Have there been times when you have brought lip service to God without really meaning what you were saying?

There was a time when someone very close to me had hurt my feelings just at the start of our Sunday morning church service. Maybe it was my pride that was hurt; but nevertheless, I was having a hard time being sincere in the words I was singing. That was one of the most difficult services I can remember. Do you know why? It wasn't due to the fact that I had been hurt by a close friend. No, the reason I had such a difficult time was because I wasn't giving my best to God. It was because whether I feel good or not, God is always good. I was focusing on other things rather than focusing completely upon Him. When we do this, we are not offering our best to God.

As I said in an earlier chapter, sometimes pushing in closer to God will cost us something. There will be times when it is easy to praise and worship God; but there will also be times when it is more difficult. Be willing to offer God the very best you have to give!

Lord, forgive me for offering you anything less than my very best! Help me, Holy Spirit, to offer the very best I have to God! In Jesus' Name!

DAY TWENTY-FIVE

*"So let us come boldly to the throne of our gracious God.
There we will receive mercy, and we will find grace to help us
when we need it most."*
Hebrews 4:16 NLT

What an invitation! We are bid to come *boldly* before the
throne of God! How many kings have given you that amazing
opportunity? And this is not just any king. This is *the* King!
When we stop and think about the incredible honor this is it
makes you wonder why in the world we don't take the
opportunity more often.

You see, there was a time when we would not have been
able to come into the Presence of the Lord. That was reserved
only for the High Priest. There was a veil in the temple that
separated the created from their Creator. But then Jesus came.

When Jesus took on death for us, the veil that once separated
us from God was torn! Because of the death and resurrection
of Christ we have been made kings and priests of God. We
have been given the privilege of coming before God *boldly*!

It makes one wonder why we don't take advantage of the
opportunity given to us. Maybe we still feel that we don't have
the right because we have not reached perfection yet. I can tell
you this, we will not reach perfection in this lifetime. So, what

are you waiting for? An invitation has been extended and your God is waiting for you to come running into His throne room! I dare you to throw caution to the wind today and run boldly to God! Fall down before Him and let Him know how much you love Him! His Word tells us that when we do such we will receive mercy and grace to help us along our way.

Father, here I am! I come boldly before Your throne today! I love you and I know You love me, too! Thank you for inviting me into Your wonderful Presence!

DAY TWENTY-SIX

"But the LORD said to Samuel, 'Don't judge by his appearance or height, for I have rejected him. The LORD doesn't see things the way you see them. People judge by outward appearance, but the LORD looks at the heart.'"
1 Samuel 16:7 NLT

David wasn't what Samuel had in mind to be the next king of Israel; but he was *exactly* who God had in mind and was just the man for the job. You see, God sees past any pretense. He looks beyond the image that we present to the world and looks intently at the heart of the matter—the heart of man.

I am going to give you a scenario that is far too familiar to many church-goers. Maybe you will be able to relate.

Bill and Nancy have been married for many years now. They have three young children, all boys, who fight almost constantly. Bill and Nancy have had their problems through the years. They have no plan to ever separate or divorce, but they have been emotionally separated for quite some time. Did I mention that they are very active in their church? Sunday rolls around again and the family pile into their SUV and head off toward the church.

The couple argues the entire length of the trip between their home and the church. The only break in the bickering and arguing comes when they need to yell at the boys who are fighting in the backseat.

When they finally arrive at the church they are nearly exhausted from the fight. They paint on fake smiles and begin to greet their fellow attendees. When the music starts Bill and Nancy are the first to clap, raise their hands, and lift their voices in song. While all of this is going on externally, Bill's mind is focused on whether they will make it out in time to catch the start of the game. Nancy on the other hand, is thinking about how annoying Bill is and wonders how the man she thought was so great turned out to be such a dud!

After the service ends Bill, Nancy, and the boys bid everyone goodbye and then get back into the car where the arguing continues. Although they put on a great show at church, behind closed doors the truth comes out. They may have everyone else fooled but God (the One Who truly matters) is no fool and can see beyond their façade. You see, He sees past the outward appearance and looks at our hearts. He knows when our worship is sincere and He knows when it is not.

Hopefully this isn't a picture of your family, but it is a story that plays out far too often. Many people go to church to keep up appearances, to expand their businesses, to catch up on the latest gossip, or to be entertained. Take a minute and begin to examine your own heart. Why do you go to church? Don't give the prepared, perfect answer but be honest with yourself and with God.

When we put on a "show" for others and then try to pass it off as worship we are greatly offending God. When this happens, we are worshiping ourselves. Whenever we do anything in the Name of the Lord for our own gain, we are taking that Name in vain and worshiping ourselves. That is a dangerous thing to do. God will not be mocked. Anything that exalts itself above Him will be cast down.

When we lift our hands in worship we must be very thoughtful of who we are really worshiping. Are we doing it for a show? God says in His Word that he hates that kind of worship. He rejects it.

When we come before Him we must make sure that we are coming before *Him* and not before our neighbors and ourselves. We must be sure that we are worshiping God alone.

God, examine my heart. I want my motives to be pure and right. If there is anything within that is making my worship of

You of no effect, then please help me to cooperate with You in fixing it.

DAY TWENTY-SEVEN

*"yet I will rejoice in the LORD! I will be joyful in the God of
my salvation!"*
Habakkuk 3:18 NLT

Life happens! No matter who you are or what you do, you
will have to face one thing or another at some point in your
life! The Bible says that it rains on the just and the unjust
alike. Although we will face things that we may not like or
understand, we can be sure that God is still to be praised during
these times.

God's goodness and worthiness isn't dependent upon our
circumstances. He is always good, always reigning, always in
control, always almighty. Always.

I want to encourage you to make the decision to rejoice in
the Lord at all times! Don't wait until you feel like it. Don't
wait until everything adds up just right. Don't wait until you
have reached a certain level of "spirituality". Praise Him now!
When we learn to praise Him when we don't feel "right" He
will see and know that our desire is to honor Him above all
else!

Are you courageous enough to say, like Habakkuk, "Even
though everything around me is a mess, I know that you are

still God! Even though I may not feel like it, I will praise You nonetheless. When things seem to be falling apart, *yet I will rejoice in the Lord!* No matter my circumstance, *I will be joyful in the God of my salvation!"*

Father, whether I feel like it or not; I will praise You!

DAY TWENTY-EIGHT

"Yours, O LORD, is the greatness, the power, the glory, the victory, and the majesty. Everything in the heavens and on earth is yours, O LORD, and this is your kingdom. We adore you as the one who is over all things."
1 Chronicles 29:11

God is many things to us. He is our father, healer, redeemer, savior, friend, etc. But we must never forget that beyond all of this He is our King and we are subjects of His kingdom.

In contrast to some other areas in the world, I don't feel that we in America have quite the understanding of what it means to be royal. We have such watered-down ideas of royalty and what that entails. We have images in our head of Cinderella, Snow White, and other Disney-esque princesses. We don't always have a grip on the realization that being royal means majestic power. Our God is not only a trusted friend—He is also the King of Kings and should be honored as such.

We are to bow before royalty. We must always be willing to humble ourselves before Him. We should be in awe of His Almighty nature. We should have a reverential fear of our King.

Too many times we try to make Him a subject of our kingdom. We sacrifice at the altar of self and bow to no one—even God. We must come to realize the truth that God is our King and we must bow to Him. He is the only King worthy. He is most holy, and we must not forget that. We are subjects of God's kingdom and the quicker you come to understand this, the better off you will be.

Today, take some time and humble yourself before your King. Honor Him as such. This is His kingdom and He is over all things.

I bow before you, my King! Everything belongs to you. I am Yours and this is Your kingdom. May I adore You as the One Who is over all things!

DAY TWENTY-NINE

*"For everything comes from him and exists by his power and is
intended for his glory. All glory to him forever! Amen."*
Romans 11:36 NLT

Everything that was created was created for the glory of God;
that includes you! We were created to bring glory to Him. He
didn't just mistakenly make you. You were created and
fashioned in a way that brings glory to God!

We should never get down on ourselves and think that we
don't matter. God doesn't make mistakes and you are not a
mistake! He created you so that you could bring glory to Him.
One sure-fire way of bringing glory to Him is by worshiping
Him!

We were created to worship Him! When we fail to do so we
are failing to bring glory to Him and we are failing to fulfill
one of our main purposes of existing!

We sometimes misplace our worship, as I have said in
earlier chapters. Sometimes we worship sports. Some of us
worship fashion. Some people worship pop-culture. But we
weren't created to worship those things and when we do so we
are living a life out of balance. We were created to worship
God!

We must strive to live a lifestyle of worship toward Him.
Many people don't like that last phrase, but the Bible is very

clear that we are to be living sacrifices unto God. In layman's terms that means "living a lifestyle of worship unto God."

Let's live our lives in a way that brings glory unto God. Let us worship God daily, not only on Sunday. Everything under the sun (and beyond) was intended for His glory—and that includes you!

You created everything, and I exist by Your power and am intended to bring You glory. May I be one who brings You glory in my life!

DAY THIRTY

"Let everything that breathes sing praises to the LORD! Praise the LORD!"
Psalm 150:6 NLT

Throughout scripture we see the call to praise the Lord! If you notice, it never says to praise Him if you feel like it. It never says to praise Him if everything in your life is perfect. It isn't some mild suggestion. It is a proclamation from our God. Let *everything* that has breath *praise the Lord!*

During our journey together I have tried to point out certain things. One of them is that we serve a God Who is holy and worthy of praise. The other is that He is still worthy when things don't always seem to be going our way.

Whether you are rich, poor, somewhere in the middle, etc., take the time to praise the Lord! I can assure you that we benefit so much from it in our lives! Praise lifts our spirits, defeats our enemies, strengthens us, and so much more! And did I mention the fact that God deserves our praise?

As you go throughout your day today, take the time to praise God. If you work in an environment where it is impossible to do it loudly then do it under your breath. Find a place where you can go to be alone during a break, or even a trip to the restroom, and praise God for all that He has done, is doing, and will do! He is worthy of praise!

Praise the Lord, Who is holy and worthy of all praise, honor, and glory! I do not want a rock to cry out in my place! Praise the Lord!

CONCLUSION

Thank you for taking this journey with me! I hope that it has inspired you to press in farther into the Presence of God! There are many more scriptures pertaining to praise and worship in the Bible. I have only included the ones that I felt led to write about. I would like to encourage you to take the time to study them out. I would also like to encourage you to not stop at day 30! Keep on worshiping God in your own prayer closet!

Revelation 4 tells us that worship continues day and night (hence, the title of this book) in Heaven. All of Heaven bows before the throne. Don't you want to join with them? It is never too early to learn how to worship God. Make it your daily practice because at some point it *will* be your daily practice!

Again, thank you for joining me on this journey! May we bring honor and glory to God all the days of our lives!

Blessings,
Justin McGowan

Made in the USA
Middletown, DE
20 February 2023

24709613R00057